TSUNAMI ALERT!

Niki Walker

Crabtree Publishing Company
www.crabtreebooks.com

DISASTER ALERT!

presented by:

Crabtree Publishing Company

www.crabtreebooks.com

Coordinating editor: Ellen Rodger

Project editor: Rachel Eagen

Editors: Carrie Gleason, Adrianna Morganelli

Book design and production coordinator: Rosie Gowsell

Layout and production assistant: Samara Parent

Scanning technician: Arlene Arch-Wilson

Art Director: Rob MacGregor

Photo research: Allison Napier

Consultants: Delores Clark, Barry Hirshorn, and Linda Sjogren, from the National Oceanic and Atmospheric Administration (NOAA)

Photographs: AP/Wide World Photos: p. 4, p. 8, p. 17, p. 18, p. 19, p. 20, p. 23 (top), p. 25, p. 26; Luis Ascui/ Reuters/ Corbis: p. 3; Babu/ Reuters/ Corbis: p. 16; Beawiharta/ Reuters/ Corbis: p. 1; Lloyd Cluff/ Corbis: p. 15; Corbis: p. 22, p. 23 (bottom); Digital Global/ Zuma/ Corbis: p. 7 (top); Benjamin Lowy/ Corbis: cover; Musee Guimet, Paris, France, Giraudon/ Bridgeman Art Library: p. 12; Yuriko Nakao/ Reuters/ Corbis: p. 7 (bottom); Sol Neelman/ Zuma/ Corbis: p. 21; Connie Ricca/ Corbis: p. 29; Darren Whiteside/ Reuters/ Corbis: p. 27 (top); AFP/AFP/ Getty Images: p. 6; Paula Bronstein/ Getty Images: p. 27 (bottom); John Russell/ AFP/ Getty Images: p. 28; David Hardy/ Photo Researchers, Inc: p. 5

Illustrations: Jim Chernishenko: p. 15, p. 24; Dan Pressman: pp. 10-11, p. 13 (all); David Wysotski, Allure Illustrations: pp. 30-31

Cover: A man surveys the damage after a large tsunami devastated South Asia in 2004.

Contents: A man grieves among the rubble of a destroyed coastline after a tsunami washed out homes and other structures.

Title page: Elephants were used to help clean up after the South Asian tsunami disaster of 2004. Elephants can use their trunks to get into small spaces that humans cannot.

Crabtree Publishing Company

www.crabtreebooks.com   1-800-387-7650

Cataloging-in-Publication Data
Walker, Niki, 1972-
  Tsunami alert! / written by Niki Walker.
      p. cm. -- (Disaster alert!)
  Includes index.
  ISBN-13: 978-0-7787-1582-5 (rlb)
  ISBN-10: 0-7787-1582-5 (rlb)
  ISBN-13: 978-0-7787-1614-3 (pb)
  ISBN-10: 0-7787-1614-7 (pb)
  1. Tsunamis--Juvenile literature. I. Title. II. Series.
  GC221.5.W36 2005
  551.46'37--dc22
                                                2005015431
                                                LC

**Published in
the United States**
PMB 16A
350 Fifth Ave.
Suite 3308
New York, NY
10118

**Published
in Canada**
616 Welland Ave.
St. Catharines
Ontario, Canada
L2M 5V6

**Published in the
United Kingdom**
73 Lime Walk
Headington
Oxford
OX3 7AD
United Kingdom

**Published
in Australia**
386 Mt. Alexander Rd.
Ascot Vale (Melbourne)
VIC 3032

Table of Contents

4   **Deadly Waves**

6   **What is a Tsunami?**

8   **Wave Science**

10   **Life of a Tsunami**

12   **Triggering Tsunamis**

16   **Slamming the Shore**

18   **Tsunami Alert!**

20   **Studying Tsunamis**

22   **Famous Tsunamis**

24   **Disaster in South Asia**

26   **The Aftermath**

28   **Staying Safe**

30   **Recipe for Disaster**

32   **Glossary and Index**

Deadly Waves

Tsunamis are the fastest, most powerful, and most destructive water waves on Earth. They can strike with little or no warning, hitting coastlines with the force of massive bombs. The waves plow across the land, flattening buildings, scattering debris for miles, and erasing whole villages.

Banda Aceh, Indonesia, 2004

People wade through flooded streets after an enormous tsunami in Southeast Asia. The tsunami was one of the worst ever recorded.

What is a disaster?
A disaster is a destructive event that affects the natural world and human communities. Some disasters are predictable, but others occur without warning. Coping successfully with a disaster depends on a community's preparation.

Harbor waves

The word tsunami comes from two Japanese words, *tsu* meaning harbor and *nami* meaning waves. The waves are named after harbors because that is where tsunamis are most often observed and are most destructive, especially in Japan, where there are many earthquakes. Tsunami waves are barely noticeable in the open ocean. The English term tidal waves is an inaccurate term to describe tsunamis, because tsunamis have nothing to do with the ocean's tides. Tides are the regular, daily rise and fall in water levels while tsunamis are rare, irregular events.

The Legend of Atlantis

The legend of Atlantis tells of a beautiful island that the gods sank under the ocean thousands of years ago. Scientists have uncovered evidence to prove the ancient story was based on the destruction of a real island. The powerful Minoan empire, in the Aegean Sea, suddenly disappeared about 3,500 years ago, when a volcano on the island of Thera erupted and collapsed into the sea. The eruption caused a tsunami that destroyed towns and villages on the Minoan island of Crete.

The story of Atlantis has been retold in books and movies, but scientists believe that a real earthquake destroyed the island Thera and caused a massive tsunami.

What is a Tsunami?

Tsunamis are rare natural disasters. There are about four tsunamis in the world each year, but they do not usually cause a lot of damage or take human lives. Major, destructive tsunamis happen about once every ten to twelve years, when a massive amount of ocean water is displaced.

Krabi, Thailand, 2004

Ocean out of balance

A tsunami is a series of waves that result from another ocean event, such as an underwater earthquake or the eruption of an underwater volcano. Both of these events cause a large amount of water to move, sending waves speeding out in all directions. The ocean tries to remain in a state of balance, called **equilibrium**. When a large **volume** of water suddenly moves, ripples, or waves, form on the surface of the ocean, moving away from the place where the water was disrupted. Close to shore, tsunami waves build on each other and rush over the land in a fast-moving flood of water. Tsunami waves may last up to several hours before the surface of the ocean is calm again, or regains equilibrium.

In some ways, a tsunami is like dropping a bar of soap into a bathtub full of water. The soap displaces some of the water, causing it to slosh over the edges of the tub. The ripples eventually get smaller and smaller as the water in the tub returns to a state of equilibrium.

Near and far

Tsunamis can be local or distant, depending on how far the source of the waves is from shore. Local tsunamis strike shores less than 60 miles (100 kilometers) from the source. Distant tsunamis travel at least 600 miles (1,000 kilometers) from their source. Teletsunamis are ocean-wide events that move from one side of an ocean to the other. Teletsunamis create local and distant tsunamis. The local tsunamis strike coasts closest to the source, while distant tsunamis race in the opposite direction, hitting faraway shores. Teletsunamis come from the same place, but damage several different coasts.

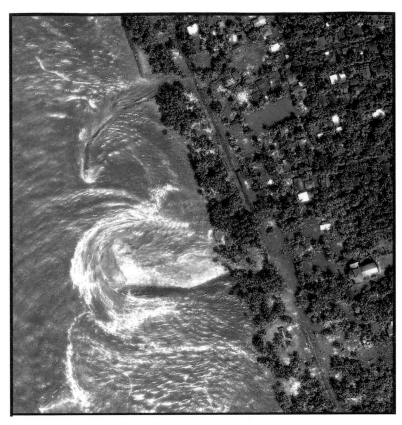

(above) An aerial shot of a tsunami pulling back out to sea in Kalutara, Sri Lanka.

(above) The costs of cleaning up and rebuilding communities after a tsunami can be overwhelming. Help from the international community is crucial after such a large-scale disaster.

Wave Science

Tsunami waves have a few things in common with regular ocean waves, but they also have several differences. The differences are what make tsunamis so powerful and destructive.

Longer and stronger

Waves are the movement of energy. All waves lose energy as they travel. The amount of energy that a wave loses depends on its wavelength. The shorter the wavelength, the more energy a wave loses. Tsunamis have very long wavelengths, so they hardly lose any energy as they travel, and reach shores with a great deal of force. Tsunamis travel so quickly once they reach shore that people cannot outrun them. Regular ocean waves created by the wind have much shorter wavelengths, lose more energy as they travel, and hit shores with much less force than tsunamis.

What's the difference?

The main differences between tsunami waves and normal ocean waves are size, speed, and how they are created. Normal ocean waves are usually between one to 16 feet (0.3 to five meters) tall. They have an average speed of 35 miles per hour (56 km/h) but can reach up to 60 miles per hour (100 km/h). Their wavelengths are usually from 130 to 1,300 feet (40 to 400 meters). Tsunami waves have much longer wavelengths, from 12 to 180 miles (20 to 300 kilometers), and in the open ocean they travel very fast, between 500 and 600 miles per hour (800 to 1,000 km/h).

Penang, Malaysia, 2004

Fierce storms create waves that are up to 18 feet (5.5 meters) tall when they hit the shore. In contrast, most tsunami waves are about 30 feet (9 meters) high as they reach shore.

The crest is the highest point of the wave.

The trough is the dip between crests. It is the lowest point of the wave.

The amplitude of the wave is the distance between the crest and the trough of the wave.

What's in a wave?

Wavelength is the distance between one crest and the next. The wave's period is the time it takes for two crests to pass the same point, such as a weather buoy. Scientists describe tsunamis as shallow-water waves. These kinds of waves have very long wavelengths compared to the depth of the water in which they travel. In the open ocean, the water is an average of 2.5 miles (four kilometers) deep. The wavelength of a tsunami is from 12 to 180 miles (20 to 300 kilometers).

Life of a Tsunami

A tsunami is a series of waves with massive wavelengths. The waves are barely noticeable in the open ocean, but they grow larger in shallow water near coasts.

Underwater disturbance

A tsunami begins when an underwater disturbance suddenly displaces a column of ocean water. This abrupt movement may be caused by an underwater volcano, landslide, or earthquake. The sudden movement releases energy throughout the water, creating waves.

Across the ocean

Tsunami waves in the open ocean are difficult to see because their long wavelengths stretch them out and keep them low. They are often less than a few feet high, but they move very quickly. People in boats might feel a tsunami wave as a sudden roll as it passes under the boat. When a tsunami wave reaches shallower water, the bottom of the wave begins to drag along the ocean floor. The wave slows down, but the water behind it continues to move quickly. The water starts to pile up, and the wave grows taller. Tsunami waves may reach heights of 30 to 100 feet (ten to 30 meters) or more as they reach the shore.

Volcanoes can create local tsunamis. Local tsunamis can be destructive to the area they strike but are not powerful enough to travel across the entire ocean.

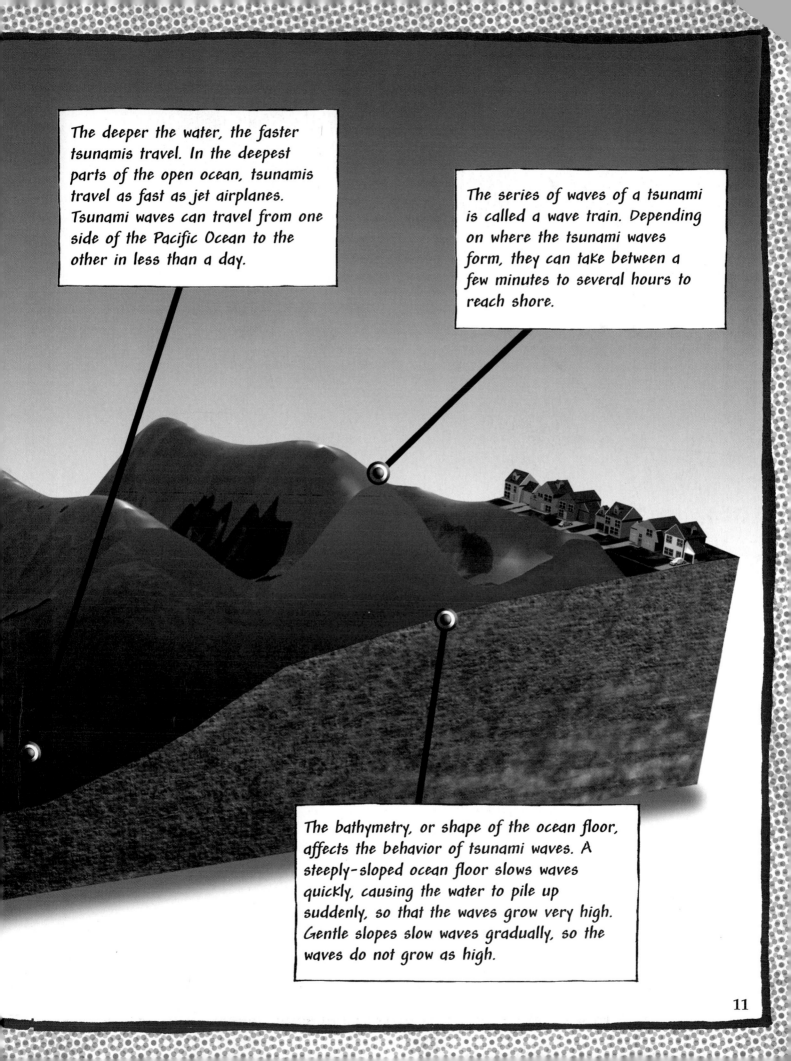

The deeper the water, the faster tsunamis travel. In the deepest parts of the open ocean, tsunamis travel as fast as jet airplanes. Tsunami waves can travel from one side of the Pacific Ocean to the other in less than a day.

The series of waves of a tsunami is called a wave train. Depending on where the tsunami waves form, they can take between a few minutes to several hours to reach shore.

The bathymetry, or shape of the ocean floor, affects the behavior of tsunami waves. A steeply-sloped ocean floor slows waves quickly, causing the water to pile up suddenly, so that the waves grow very high. Gentle slopes slow waves gradually, so the waves do not grow as high.

Triggering Tsunamis

A few events in nature have enough power to displace massive amounts of water and create tsunamis. These events include earthquakes, volcanoes, landslides, and asteroid crashes. Any event that creates a tsunami is described as tsunamigenic.

Earthquakes

The Earth's crust is made up of moving slabs called **plates**. The plates move about an inch or two (2.5 to five centimeters) each year. Some plates move away from one another, some scrape past each other, and others crunch directly into each other. The plates do not move against each other easily. They stick in many places, and energy builds there. In time, the two plate edges finally snap, creating an earthquake as they release the built-up energy.

The Richter Scale

The Richter Scale is a system for measuring the size of earthquakes. It was developed in the 1930s by the **seismologist** Charles F. Richter. The scale rates earthquakes from one to ten, based on the amount of ground motion, or shaking, caused by the earthquake. New instruments developed since the 1930s have made it possible to record many other earthquake characteristics, but the Richter Scale is still used to compare relative sizes of earthquakes. The **magnitude** of an earthquake does not measure how damaging it is. An earthquake's destruction depends on factors such as how near to cities the earthquake occurs, the materials used to build structures, and the physical features of the landscape in the area.

This Japanese painting shows a tsunami as large, towering waves, but tsunami waves do not build until they reach shore.

Seismic tsunami

Earthquakes are the cause of almost all tsunamis, but not all earthquakes trigger tsunamis. Underwater earthquakes are more likely to cause large tsunamis that travel across the entire ocean.

Earthquakes near coasts can cause tsunamis, too. An underwater earthquake is likely to cause a tsunami if it is large, it happens near the ocean floor rather than far below it, and it causes part of the ocean floor to heave up or drop down.

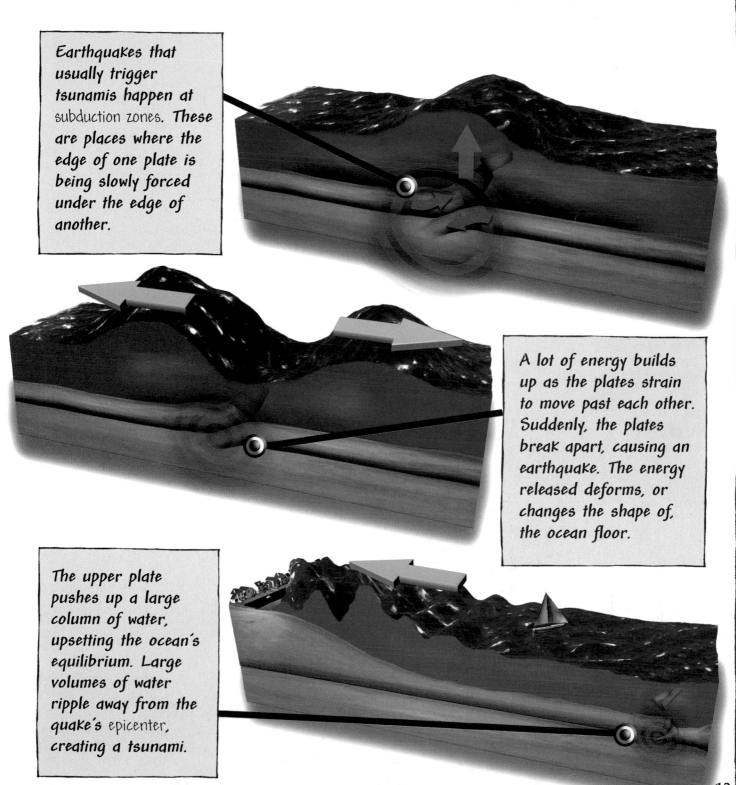

Earthquakes that usually trigger tsunamis happen at subduction zones. These are places where the edge of one plate is being slowly forced under the edge of another.

A lot of energy builds up as the plates strain to move past each other. Suddenly, the plates break apart, causing an earthquake. The energy released deforms, or changes the shape of, the ocean floor.

The upper plate pushes up a large column of water, upsetting the ocean's equilibrium. Large volumes of water ripple away from the quake's epicenter, creating a tsunami.

Volcanoes

Volcanoes form where cracks in the Earth's surface release gas and lava, or melted rock. They usually form along the edges of the Earth's plates. Volcanoes can trigger tsunamis in two ways. When a volcano located near shore erupts with a violent blast, it can blow out part of its side, sending tons of rock and lava into the nearby ocean and displacing a lot of water. Volcanoes can also trigger tsunamis by dumping a lot of lava into a nearby ocean very quickly. An underwater volcano can trigger a tsunami when it suddenly releases a lot of gas with a great deal of force. The gas blows up toward the ocean's surface, displacing a large volume of water and creating tsunami waves at the surface of the ocean.

Asteroid impacts

An asteroid could cause a tsunami by crashing into the ocean and displacing a large volume of water. This has never been recorded in human history, but some **geologists** are certain that this has happened in the past. They believe that an asteroid crashed into present-day Mexico 65 million years ago and caused the dinosaurs to become extinct. These scientists believe that this asteroid triggered major tsunamis in several parts of the world.

Volcanoes close to shore can cause tsunamis when they erupt suddenly, sending a lot of rock and lava into the ocean and displacing massive amounts of water.

Lituya Bay, Alaska, 14 years after a 8.0 magnitude earthquake. The earthquake caused a large landslide that hit the bay, causing the run-up, or rise in the water level, to reach 1,720 feet (524 meters).

Landslides

Landslides happen when a large amount of rock or dirt comes loose from the side of a mountain or cliff and tumbles downhill. Landslides happen above the water, but they also happen in the ocean, where there are underwater mountains. The falling rock and dirt suddenly displaces a lot of water, creating a tsunami. Landslides are often triggered by underwater earthquakes. These landslides, together with the force of the quake, can cause major tsunamis.

Most tsunamis occur in the Pacific Ocean, in an area known as the "Ring of Fire." Many subduction zones in the region cause it to be home to more than half of the world's volcanoes, and almost all major earthquakes.

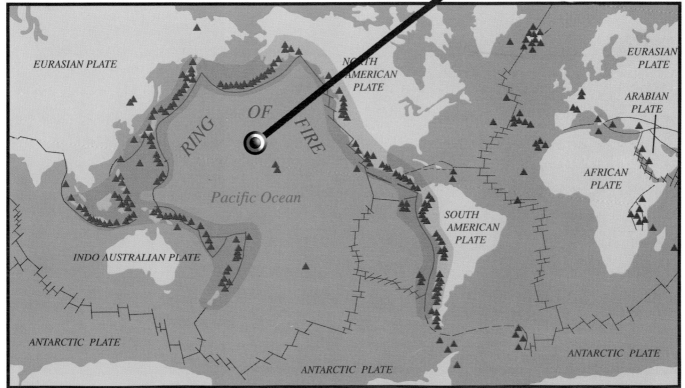

Slamming the Shore

Tsunamis roar into coasts with a force and fury that is hard to imagine. The waves snap trees, destroy roads and bridges, smash or move buildings, and toss cars and ships around like toys. Tsunamis can also shatter coral reefs and erase beaches.

Madras, India, 2004

Unpredictable arrivals

Tsunamis are always made up of more than one wave, but no one knows how many waves will arrive or how much time will pass between them. The waves may be ten minutes or more than an hour apart. No one knows which wave will be the most destructive. Usually, the first wave is not the largest or most powerful. Later waves are often more dangerous, not only because they are greater in size, but also because they swirl around the debris left from earlier waves, striking buildings and destroying structures.

Rushing in

Not all tsunamis look the same as they arrive on shore. Most tsunamis look like massive, quickly rising floods. Sometimes, tsunamis look like towering walls of water. These waves, known as **bores,** have frothing white faces, or fronts. They plow onto shore, collapse, and then race over the land in all directions for up to an hour.

Tsunami waves can strike up to an hour apart. Many people are drowned by heading to the beach before it is safe.

Traveling inland

Tsunami waves hit the shore with such power that the water may spread over a mile (1.6 kilometers) inland before it finally runs out of energy and stops. The distance tsunamis travel inland is called **inundation**. The slope of the land determines how far the water will travel. Tsunami waves can travel ten or more miles (16 or more kilometers) inland if the land is flat. The waves will **recede** back to sea if the land has a steep incline. Run-up is the height above sea level that a wave reaches on land. It is measured from the coast to the farthest point of inundation.

Some of the most devastating effects of tsunamis are caused by the debris carried by the waves, rather than the waves themselves. This boat was dropped on shore, flattening this woman's house in seconds.

Tsunami Alert!

It is difficult to predict when earthquakes and other tsunamigenic events will occur, which makes forecasting tsunamis almost impossible. Once a tsunami does form, the only way to keep people safe is to warn them that the waves are headed their way.

Tsunami Warning System

There are two tsunami warning centers in the U.S.: the Pacific Tsunami Warning Center (PTWC) in Hawaii, and the West Coast/Alaska Tsunami Warning Center in Alaska. Scientists monitor a network of seismographs, **tide gauges,** and **deep-ocean detectors** in the Pacific. Seismographs record vibrations caused by earthquakes. When a large earthquake is detected, warning centers send news bulletins to the 27 countries that belong to the International Tsunami Warning System of the Pacific Ocean.

Warnings and watches

After the countries involved in the PTWC have been alerted of a potential earthquake, scientists continue to monitor information about the quake. They have minutes to put together the seismic data and figure out if the earthquake is large enough to trigger a tsunami. If it is, tsunami warnings are sent out to the countries that will be affected. People are advised to evacuate, or leave the area. Tsunami watches are issued to countries farther away from the source, alerting them that a tsunami might strike.

Volunteers and residents evacuate after a tsunami warning is issued. Aftershocks sometimes follow an earthquake, but they are not as devastating as the initial quake.

A tsunami buoy onboard a ship belonging to the National Oceanic and Atmospheric Administration (NOAA). This device is used for measuring changes in ocean waves, which might signal a tsunami.

Better predictions

A new system of deep-ocean detectors is helping make tsunami warnings much more accurate. The system, called DART (Deep-Ocean Assessment and Reporting of Tsunamis), is made up of sensors, buoys, and **satellites**. The sensors rest on the ocean floor and record changes in the water pressure, which may signal a tsunami wave passing overhead.

The sensors can detect tsunami waves only half an inch (one centimeter) high. The sensors send data to the buoys floating on the surface. The buoys, in turn, relay the information to satellites, which then send it to monitoring centers, where scientists receive it. This system can help scientists confirm the existence of a tsunami much earlier, which allows them to issue accurate warnings much more quickly than in the past.

A computer monitors seismic activity, while a scientist tracks tsunami activity at the Tsunami Warning Center in Hawaii. Not all earthquakes cause tsunamis. Accurate equipment is important for not sending out false alarms to communities.

Studying Tsunamis

An area that has been hit by a tsunami is likely to be hit again in the future. By studying how tsunamis form, travel, and hit the shore, scientists are improving their understanding of the waves as well as their ability to predict how future tsunamis may strike.

Collecting evidence

After a tsunami has struck, teams of scientists immediately begin collecting samples for further study. They note watermarks on buildings and measure the height of debris left in trees and on roofs. They also mark plants and trees killed by seawater, the location of debris dropped by the waves, measure deposits of ocean sand, and note the location and shape of **erosion** on the shore. All of the information they gather helps them determine the tsunami's inundation and run-up, and helps them piece together a picture of the tsunami—how it moved, its speed, and its force. Besides collecting measurements and other information, scientists also speak with eyewitnesses and survivors.

Volunteer scuba divers carry away debris found in the water after a tsunami. Large pieces of floating debris, such as trees, cars, or even homes, can cause damage to coastal property. Other debris, such as nails and other sharp objects, can seriously harm people and animals on the cleanup site.

Making models

Scientists use the information they gather to create computer **models**. Models allow scientists to "see" how tsunamis behave. Scientists can also create models to show how changes in the size of the trigger, the depth, the bathymetry, and other factors would change the tsunami, its inundation, and its run-up.

The Tsunami Wave Basin at Oregon State University, where scientists from around the world study wave action. Their research helps improve systems for monitoring waves in the ocean. These people are seeing themselves in mirror-image as a wave passes in the tank.

Reducing risk

The information scientists gather about past tsunamis and the models they create can be used to make **hazard maps**. These maps show areas along coasts that are most at risk from tsunami waves. Governments can use the maps to plan escape routes and decide where to allow homes, schools, and other buildings to be constructed.

Wave tanks

Some scientists use wave tanks to create miniature versions of tsunamis and study their behavior. They can trigger model landslides and other tsunamigenic events to observe the waves they create and how the waves behave.

Famous Tsunamis

Tsunamis have been striking coasts for as long as there have been oceans. A few tsunamis have stood out for their size or for the incredible damage they caused.

Krakatoa

On August 26, 1883, a volcano on the island of Krakatoa, Indonesia, violently exploded. It was one of the biggest volcanic blasts in history. People as far away as Australia heard the explosion, which blew apart the volcano and caused most of the island to collapse into the ocean. This collapse triggered tsunamis up to 131 feet (40 meters) high. The tsunamis swept across the islands of Java and Sumatra and killed more than 36,000 people.

Japan's worst tsunamis

Japan has been hit by more tsunamis than any other country, and many have been among the biggest in history. On June 15, 1896, more than 27,000 people were killed when a tsunami more than 80 feet (25 meters) high swept away boats and villages along the coast of Sanriku. The worst tsunami in Japanese history happened more than a hundred years earlier. In 1707, waves struck the southeast region and killed more than 30,000 people.

The front page of a London newspaper on September 8, 1883, featured an illustration of the Krakatoa eruption, between the Indonesian islands of Java and Sumatra.

Lituya Bay, Alaska

Lituya Bay, Alaska, is a long, narrow bay surrounded by high walls of rock on all sides. On July 9, 1958, it was the site of a local tsunami of staggering height. The tsunami peaked at 1,720 feet (524 meters). The tsunami was created by a massive landslide of rocks down one of the rock walls. Two boats were sunk, and two people died.

The Chilean tsunami

On May 22, 1960, the biggest earthquake in recorded history rocked the ocean off Chile. A Pacific-wide tsunami raced away from the site of the quake. The first wave struck Chile's shore between ten and 15 minutes later. Other waves crossed the Pacific, hitting Hawaii and Japan. Over 2,000 Chileans were killed, either by the earthquake, measuring 9.5 on the Richter Scale, or in the tsunamis it created. The disaster killed 61 people in Hawaii and 122 in Japan.

(above) Despite accurate warning systems, tsunamis continue to wipe out the coasts of Japan because the disasters are hard to predict.

(below) A severe tsunami leveled Arica, Chile, in 1868. This photo was taken later, but still shows the debris left over from the disaster.

Arica, Chile

Disaster in South Asia

One of the worst natural disasters in history occurred on the morning of Decemeber 26, 2004. An earthquake in the Indian Ocean triggered the most deadly tsunami ever recorded.

Making history

The earthquake was the largest in more than 40 years. It occurred just off the coast of northern Sumatra and sent waves speeding outward at more than 500 miles per hour (800 km/h). Within 15 minutes of the earthquake, the first wave struck Sumatra. Over the next few hours, waves struck nine other unsuspecting countries. When the waves finally stopped seven hours later, towns, cities, fishing villages, and tourist resorts lay in ruins. Many thousands of people were dead, injured, or missing. Scientists are now working to develop a tsunami warning system for the Indian Ocean. It will be completed by the end of 2006.

No warning

One of the reasons the tsunami killed so many people is because there is no tsunami warning system for the Indian Ocean, as there is in the Pacific Ocean. According to the PTWC, which detected the earthquake, every attempt was made to alert the countries that were in danger, but people did not know what to do because of a lack of emergency plans in these countries. Another reason the tsunami was so deadly was because it hit during one of the busiest tourist seasons, when the beaches were packed with vacationers. When the first waves began rolling in, people on the beach had very little time to react. More than 280,000 people died or disappeared.

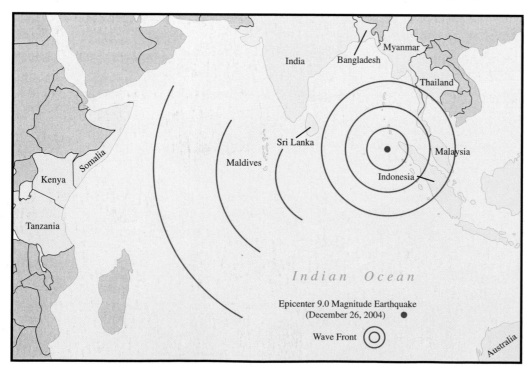

The ocean-wide tsunami hit Indonesian islands within fifteen minutes. Other waves raced more than 1,850 miles (3,000 kilometers) to strike Somalia six hours after the earthquake.

The world rallied

People around the world were shocked by news of the tsunami and by images of the destruction it caused. They rushed to help the survivors by donating money, food, clothing, and other supplies. Governments also offered money and sent soldiers and doctors to help with the cleanup, rescue, and medical treatment. The destruction was so great that, in spite of the global effort, the **United Nations** estimated that the cleanup and rebuilding would take more than four years to complete, especially in the areas that were the hardest hit.

1 The first tsunami wave comes rushing to the coast.

2 The wave strikes the coast.

3 The powerful wave destroys everything in its path.

4 The wave retreats back to sea, leaving flooded land, damaged coastline, and flattened homes.

The Aftermath

Major tsunamis leave a path of destruction in their wake as they retreat back to sea. Once the waves have stopped, people are left with the overwhelming job of clearing the wreckage, caring for the sick and injured, and trying to prevent the spread of illness.

Swept up

Tsunamis sweep up animals, boats, cars, and anything else in their path. They tear roofs off buildings, smash walls, and rip trees from the ground. People often get caught in the powerful waves, which churn them among the debris like clothes in a washing machine. When the waves move out to sea again, they drag some of what they have caught with them. People who are not swept out to sea are often injured from being struck by debris.

Picking up the pieces

Tsunamis leave piles of ocean sand and tons of wreckage. Broken glass and bricks, splintered wood, twisted metal, and uprooted trees cover the ground, making it almost impossible to travel. Overturned vehicles are found in streets or on top of buildings.

After a tsunami hits, many people are left without homes. International relief agencies often set up temporary shelters for people to live in while they try to rebuild their lives. Clearing away debris is overwhelming and exhausting work.

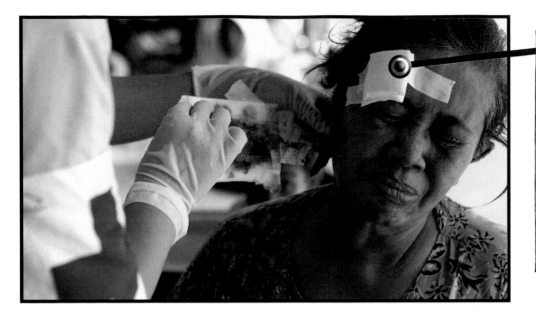

People wounded by churning debris require immediate medical attention. Volunteers set up temporary first aid stations to treat the injured.

Search and rescue

Before any cleanup begins, people search the wreckage for anyone trapped in it. Temporary clinics are often set up to give emergency care to injured people. People also work to recover the bodies of people killed by the waves. It is important that bodies are buried quickly to help prevent the spread of disease.

Destroying the food supply

Food can be scarce in the days immediately following a tsunami. Livestock are killed or swept away, and food crops may be buried under sand and water. The food in flooded kitchens, restaurants, and grocery stores may be **contaminated** by the dirty water and is no longer safe to eat.

Unhealthy conditions

Widespread illness can be a concern in the days and weeks after a tsunami. People left homeless by the disaster are crowded into shelters, where waterborne illnesses and diseases spread by bacteria can spread quickly. Tsunami waves often break water and sewage pipes, flooding reservoirs and wells with dirty water. People become dehydrated and weak in towns and cities left without clean drinking water, and those who do drink unclean water become very sick.

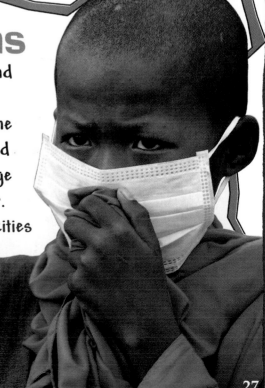

Breathing masks help filter out pollutants that are kicked up into the air during cleanup.

Staying Safe

Towns and cities near coastlines have emergency plans for dealing with tsunamis. People in those areas can improve their chances of surviving by knowing who to listen to, where to go, and what to do.

Koh Raya, Thailand, 2004

Away from the waves

The best way to survive a tsunami is to avoid it completely by heading for higher ground away from the coast. As soon as people hear a warning, they should begin to evacuate. Sometimes tsunamis hit so fast that people do not have a chance to evacuate. In those situations, people should head for the highest floors of sturdy, concrete buildings.

People try to outrun the first tsunami waves of the South Asian disaster. The waves crashed for over an hour, claiming over 260,000 lives, and devastating entire countries. Thousands of people were swept away by the waves and were never seen again.

Tsunami safety

Many people have been saved during tsunamis by remembering a few important things:

• When the ground shakes near a beach, it could be an earthquake, and it could mean a tsunami is coming. Get away from the beach as fast as possible.

• When the ocean suddenly pulls back from the shore, don't stop to look—head away from the beach as far and as fast as possible.

• Tsunamis are made up of several waves that may be up to an hour apart—people should never return to the coast until an official message says it is safe to do so.

TSUNAMI HAZARD ZONE

IN CASE OF EARTHQUAKE, GO TO HIGH GROUND OR INLAND

Have on hand:

People living in coastal areas should prepare an emergency kit that they can take with them when they evacuate. The kit should include:

• a battery-operated radio to hear local emergency broadcasts and updates
• a flashlight
• extra batteries
• band-aids
• bottled water
• canned food
• a hand-operated can opener

Recipe for Disaster

Here is an easy activity that allows you to see displacement in action. Watch how the waves form and how they move away from their source. When you're finished, use an old towel to wipe up any water that has spilled.

What you need:
* long, rectangular clear plastic container
* sand
* water
* pitcher
* plasticine
* miniature toy houses, trees, or people

What you need:
1. Pack the sand against one of the short sides of the container. Shape it into a slope.

2. Add the miniature houses, trees, or people to the shore. Place some of them close to the edge of the slope.

3. Using the pitcher, carefully pour water into the other end of the container, until the container is about half full. Try not to disturb the sand too much. Form three clumps of plasticine: one small, one medium, and one large. Drop the small clump into the container, near the edge without sand. Watch how waves form and travel up the sandy slope.

4. Remove the plasticine, then drop in the medium clump. Next, drop in the large clump. Watch how the waves behave for each. What do you notice?

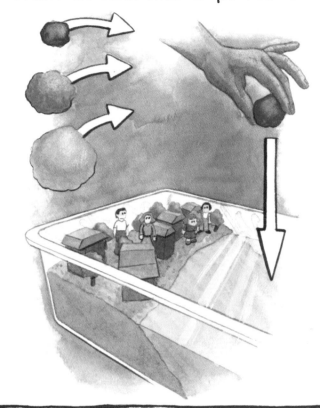

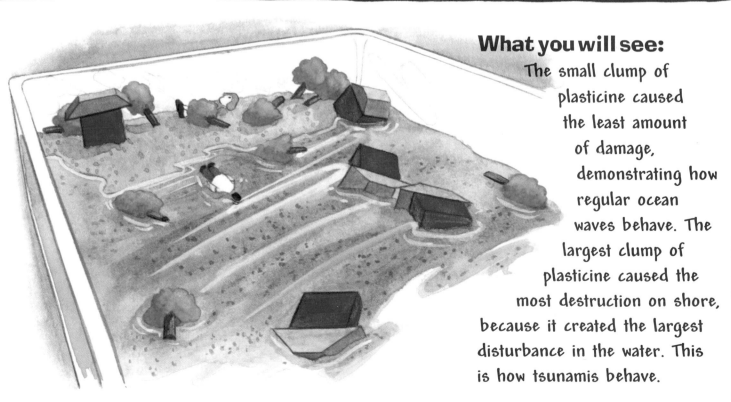

What you will see:

The small clump of plasticine caused the least amount of damage, demonstrating how regular ocean waves behave. The largest clump of plasticine caused the most destruction on shore, because it created the largest disturbance in the water. This is how tsunamis behave.

Glossary

aftershocks Smaller vibrations that follow a major earthquake

bore A fast-moving wave with a steep face

buoy A device that floats in the water and uses various instruments to record ocean data

contaminated Unclean

coral reef An ocean ridge made by small animals

debris Pieces of material that can cause damage as they are tossed around by water or wind

deep-ocean detector A sensor that sits deep in the ocean to monitor changes in the water

displaced When something is moved from its position by something else

epicenter The place on Earth located directly above the origin of an earthquake

equilibrium The state of being in balance

erosion The wearing away of soil by water or air

geologist A scientist who studies the Earth's landforms, such as mountains

hazard map A map that shows which regions are vulnerable to specific natural disasters

inundation Flooding

magnitude The size of an earthquake

model A replica of some sort of phenomenon that scientists use to study the real thing

plates The large slabs of rock that make up the Earth's surface

recede To pull back

relief agency An organization that helps communities recover from a disaster

satellite A body that orbits the Earth and takes pictures to help scientists forecast natural events

seismologist A scientist who studies earthquakes

subduction zones The places on the Earth where two plates meet

tide gauge A device that measures sea level

tsunamigenic Something that causes tsunamis

United Nations A global organization that helps to maintain peace and provide aid to countries in need

volume An amount of space taken up by something, usually a liquid

Index

amplitude 9
asteroid 12, 14

bathymetry 11
buoys 9, 19

Chile 23
crest 8

Deep-Ocean Assessment and Reporting of Tsunamis 19
distant tsunamis 7

earthquakes 5, 10, 12, 13, 15, 18, 19, 23
emergency kit 29

harbor waves 5

International Tsunami Warning System 18
inundation 17

Krakatoa 22

landslide 10, 12, 15

local tsunamis 7, 10

Pacific Tsunami Warning Center 18, 24

Richter Scale 12
Ring of Fire 15

satellite 19
shallow-water waves 8
Southeast Asia 4, 24-25, 28
subduction zone 13

teletsunamis 7
tides 5
tsunami warning, watch 18
Tsunami Wave Basin 21

volcano 6, 10, 12, 14, 15, 22

wave period 9
wave train 11
wavelength 8, 9, 10
West Coast/Alaska Tsunami Warning Center 18